Find It in Nature!

Trees

by Jenna Lee Gleisner

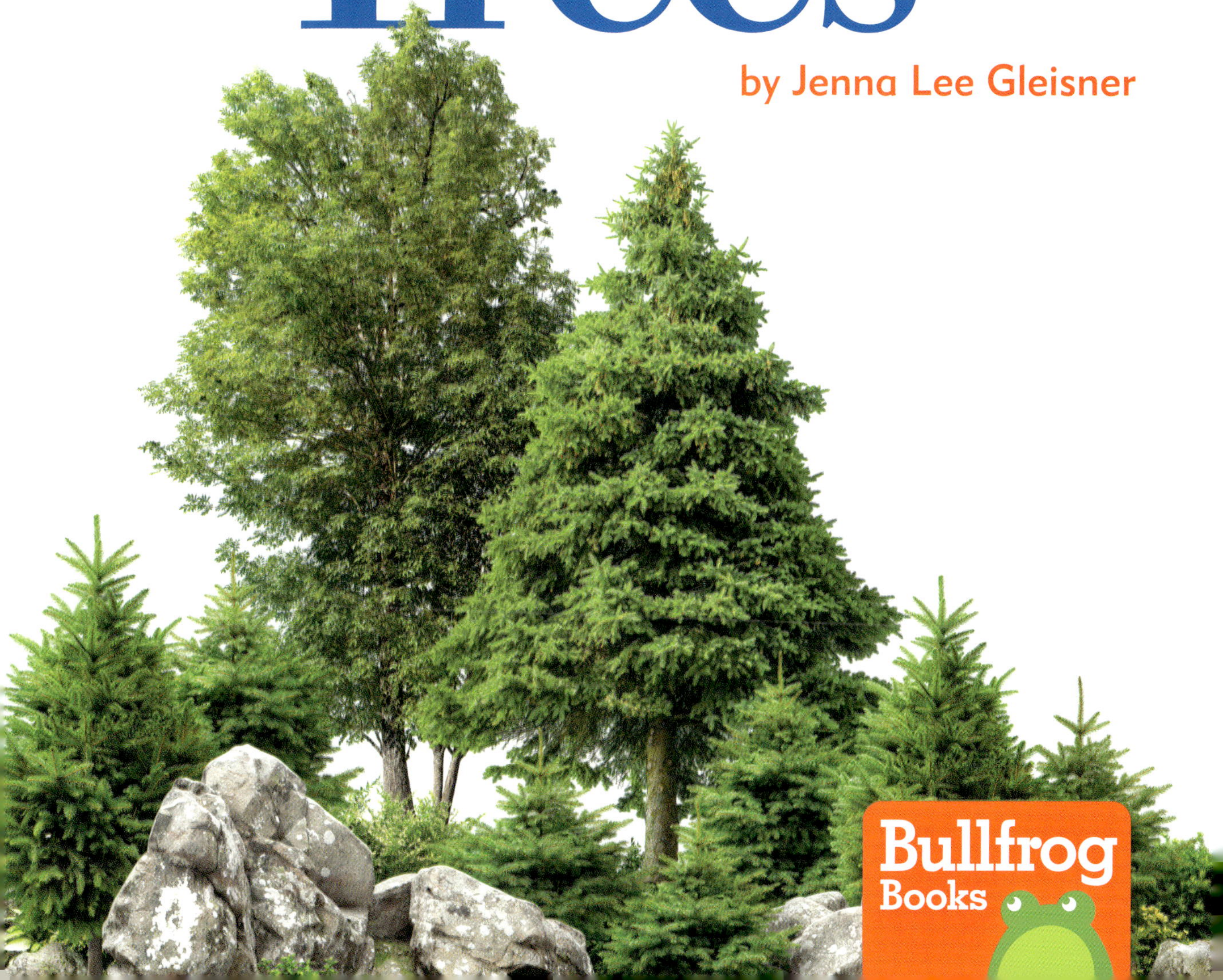

Bullfrog Books

Ideas for Parents and Teachers

Bullfrog Books let children practice reading informational text at the earliest reading levels. Repetition, familiar words, and photo labels support early readers.

Before Reading

- Discuss the cover photo. What does it tell them?
- Look at the picture glossary together. Read and discuss the words.

Read the Book

- "Walk" through the book and look at the photos. Let the child ask questions. Point out the photo labels.
- Read the book to the child, or have him or her read independently.

After Reading

- Prompt the child to think more. Ask: What trees grow near you? How do you know what kinds they are?

Bullfrog Books are published by Jump!
5357 Penn Avenue South
Minneapolis, MN 55419
www.jumplibrary.com

Library of Congress Cataloging-in-Publication Data

Names: Gleisner, Jenna Lee, author.
Title: Trees / by Jenna Lee Gleisner.
Description: Minneapolis: Jump!, Inc., 2024.
Series: Find it in nature! | Includes index.
Audience: Ages 5–8
Identifiers: LCCN 2023023807 (print)
LCCN 2023023808 (ebook)
ISBN 9798889966838 (hardcover)
ISBN 9798889966845 (paperback)
ISBN 9798889966852 (ebook)
Subjects: LCSH: Trees—Juvenile literature.
Classification: LCC QK475.8 .G56 2024 (print)
LCC QK475.8 (ebook)
DDC 582.16—dc23/eng/20230626
LC record available at https://lccn.loc.gov/2023023807
LC ebook record available at https://lccn.loc.gov/2023023808

Editor: Katie Chanez
Designer: Molly Ballanger

Photo Credits: Aksenova Natalya/Shutterstock, cover; Artiste2d3d/Shutterstock, 1; watin/Shutterstock, 3; Erick Margarita Images/Shutterstock, 4, 23tm; olko1975/Shutterstock, 5; rodho/Shutterstock, 6; Sean Pavone/iStock, 6–7; Texturis/Shutterstock, 8; fermate/iStock, 9; VladKK/Shutterstock, 10–11; romiri/Shutterstock, 11, 22tl, 23bl; Gaynor-diane/Shutterstock, 12–13, 23tr; Wirestock/Dreamstime, 14–15, 23tl; Janet Moore/Shutterstock, 15, 23bm; T.TATSU/Shutterstock, 16–17; yenwen/iStock, 18; GoShiva/Shutterstock, 19, 23br; Sait Aydin/iStock, 20–21; Lena Miava/Shutterstock, 22 (tml); Butterfly Hunter/Shutterstock, 22 (top center); Lena Pronne/Shutterstock, 22 (tmr); fotografos/Shutterstock, 22 (tr); Elena Elisseeva/Shutterstock, 22 (maple); Goinyk Production/Shutterstock, 22 (pine); BanksPhotos/iStock, 22 (willow); kosam/Shutterstock, 22 (oak); Uhryn Larysa/Shutterstock, 22 (palm); naKornCreate/Shutterstock, 24.

Printed in the United States of America at Corporate Graphics in North Mankato, Minnesota.

Table of Contents

Tree Clues

Look! A willow tree.
How do we know?
Its branches droop.

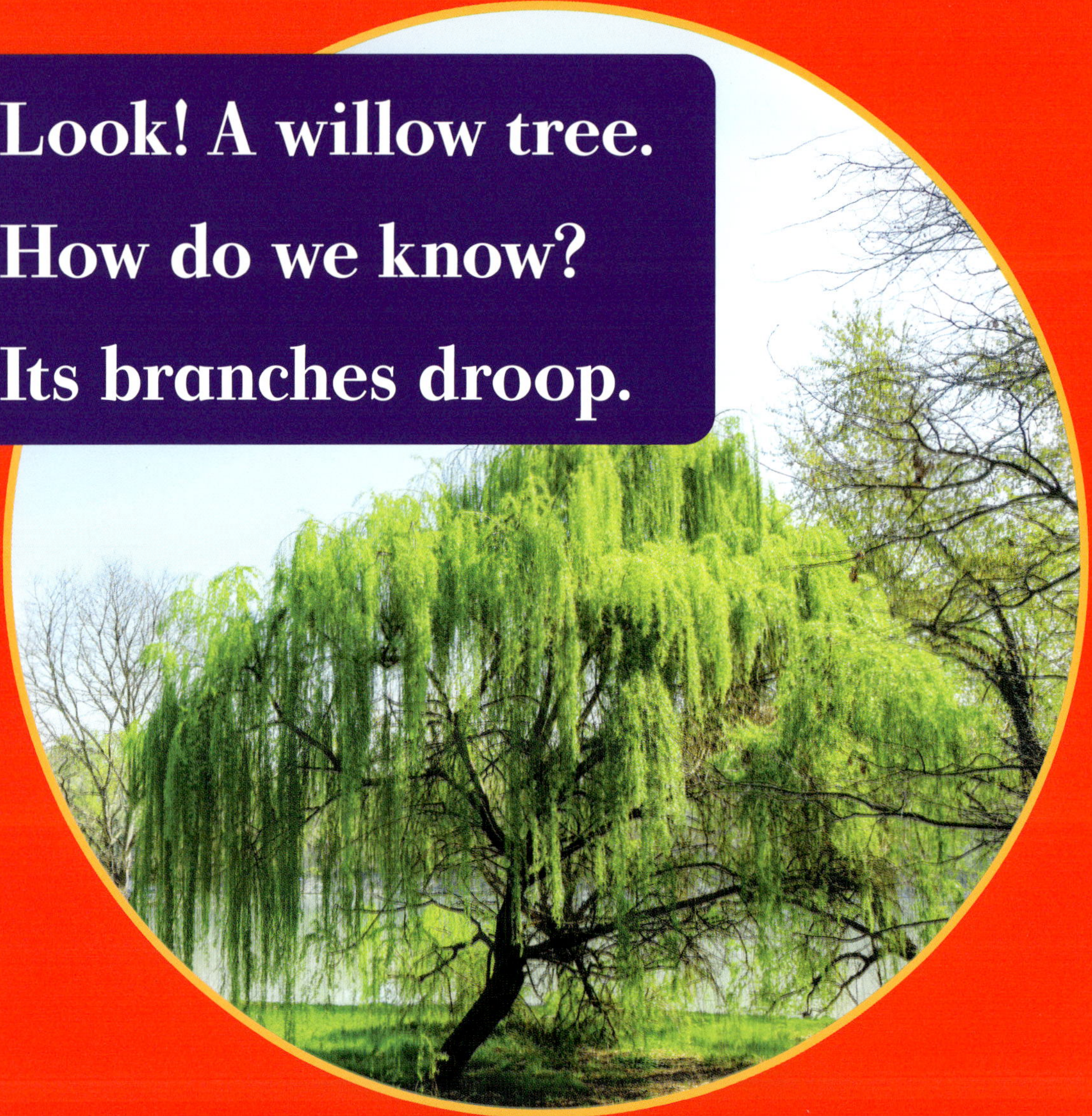

Its leaves are clues.
They are thin and green.

Palm tree leaves are long. They make fronds.

Maple tree leaves have five points, like a hand.

They turn colors.
They fall off each year.

A pine tree has needles.
It keeps them all year.

Oak tree leaves have lobes.

Nuts are clues, too.

Oak trees grow acorns.

acorn
lobe

bark

Bark is a clue.

This birch tree has white bark.

It peels.

Fruit is a clue.

Apples are ready to pick.

Yum!

Size is a clue.

Redwoods are tall.

Their trunks go straight up.

Up, up, up!

Look around.

There are many kinds of trees.

What trees grow near you?

Match the Leaf

Match each leaf to its tree. Look back at the book if you need help!

maple

pine

willow

oak

palm

Picture Glossary

bark
The tough outer covering on the trunks of trees.

droop
To hang down.

lobes
Curved or rounded shapes that stick out.

needles
Thin, pointy leaves on pine trees.

peels
Comes off in pieces or strips.

trunks
Thick, main parts of trees.

Index

To Learn More

Finding more information is as easy as 1, 2, 3.

1. Go to www.factsurfer.com
2. Enter "trees" into the search box.
3. Choose your book to see a list of websites.